Hello
I am
Caroline

Surname

My Birthday 🎂

I live in

Bookaful Press
www.bookaful.com

It's ⚡ Amazing Being CAROLINE

Make your own fun journal - packed with memories!

A self portrait by Caroline

Contents

Hey Caroline!

This is a book about you! Made by you!

There's loads of things to do with loads of spaces for you to squeeze in all the most interesting things about you..

There are plenty of opportunities for you to draw and colour and stick in pictures.

Look out for the letter to "Future Caroline" this is your opportunity to send a letter to your future self reminding them who you are and what your hope and dreams are...

Fill out this book with anything and everything you want to, then treasure it for the rest of your life...

When you look back over the coming years it will remind Caroline who Caroline is!

At the end of the book are plenty of blank pages for the stuff you couldn't fit in anywhere else!

Very strict
RULES
about filling out
this book...

You must fill out this book in any order you want...

You can use whatever materials you want.

Scribble, scrawl, colour, doodle or stick wherever the fancy takes you.

There's no right or wrong, it's your book do what you want!

Golden Rule: It's all about

CAROLINE

Have Fun!

All about Caroline

These pages are all about you, the amazing and wonderful Caroline!

Full Name ....

Height ....

Hair Colour...

Eye Colour...

Four things I love doing: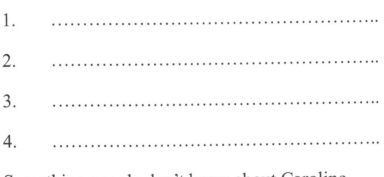

1.   ....

2.   ....

3.   ....

4.   ....

Something people don't know about Caroline

....

....

If Caroline were a character in a story,
how would the author introduce them?
Write a short description of Caroline

....

....

....

....

....

....

....

....

....

....

....

Caroline's Home

Draw a picture of your home, or you can stick in a photograph.

Caroline's Folk

Draw a picture of the folk you live with, or you can stick in a photograph.

Draw a map of Caroline's town with her road and favourite amenities...

Local Map

Key

Caroline's Favourite Local places

Restaurant

Shop

Green Place

Building or Monument

A Day in Caroline's Life

 Detail below a typical day in your life.
Write down what an average day is like.
From when you get up to what you eat,
things you do after school and what you do
before bed time.

Time	Activity

Six Things People Might Say About Caroline

Caroline & Music

What is your favourite type of music?

....

What instruments do you like or play?

....

Who are your favourite singers, groups or musicians?

1. ....

2. ....

3. ....

4. ....

5. ....

What are Caroline's five favourite songs?

1. ....

2. ....

3. ....

4. ....

5. ....

What group or singer (past or present) would you most like to see live?

If you had to make up a pop-star stage name for yourself what would it be?

Caroline's School

What is your school called?

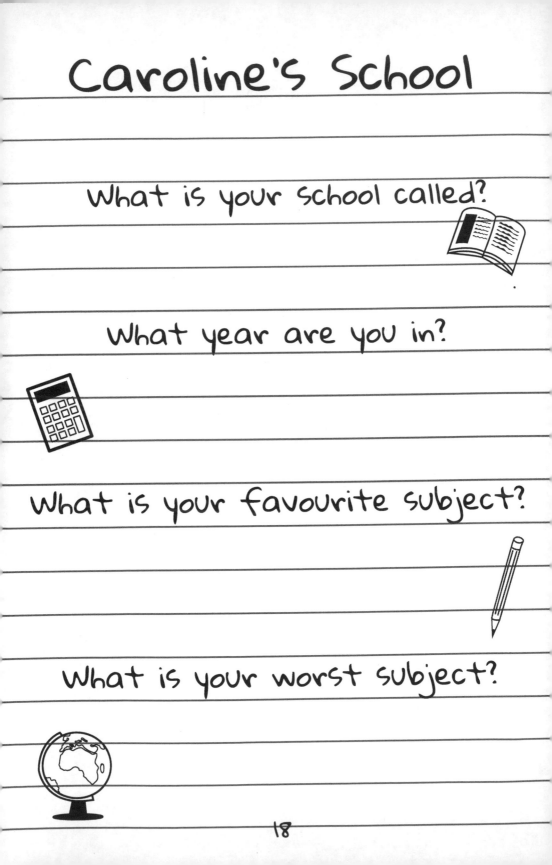

What year are you in?

What is your favourite subject?

What is your worst subject?

Who is your head teacher?

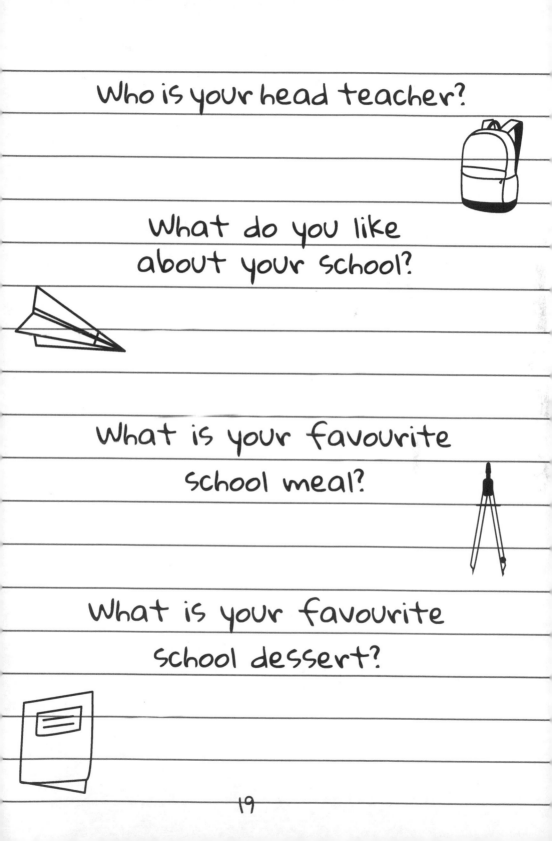

What do you like
about your school?

What is your favourite
school meal?

What is your favourite
school dessert?

Caroline's School Report!

This is your chance to *write* a school report for one of your teachers!

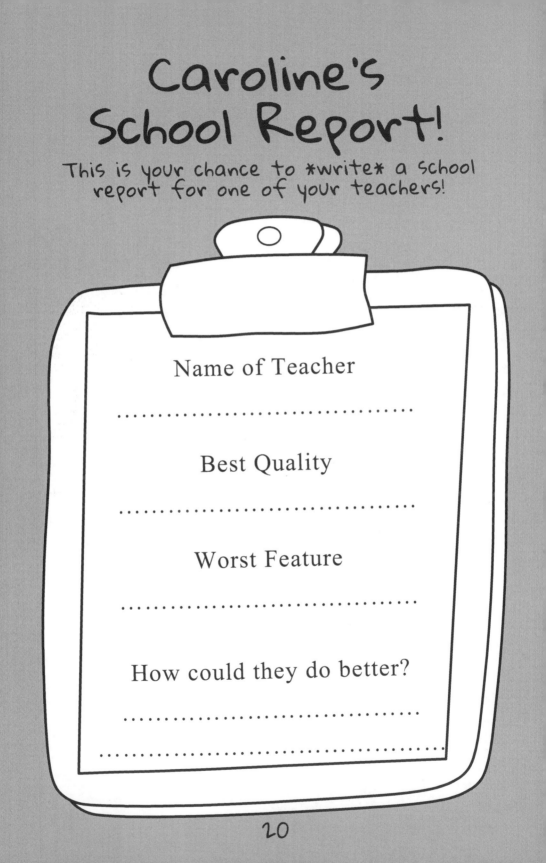

Name of Teacher

....

Best Quality

....

Worst Feature

....

How could they do better?

....

....

Rate this teacher out of 10

......

Who was your best teacher ever?

....

Best Quality?

....

Rate this teacher out of 10

.....

21

Caroline's Friends

List your friends names and write down where you met them and what you most like about them

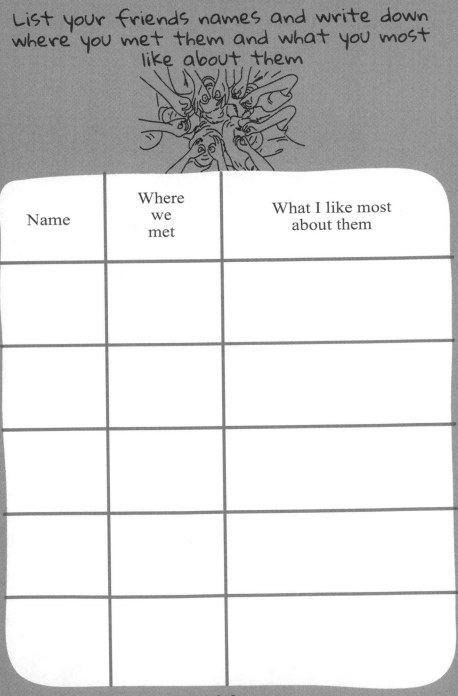

Name	Where we met	What I like most about them

Stick your favourite photo of you and your friends here or draw a picture and you can also decorate the frame.

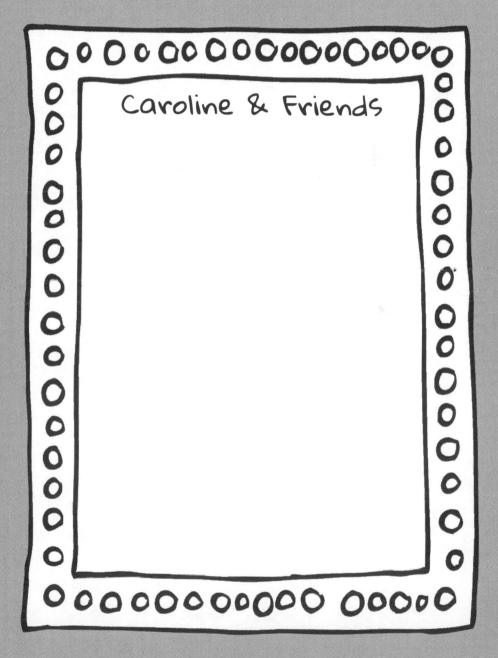

Caroline & Friends

Caroline's Perfect Friend

Use this chart to describe a real or imaginary "perfect friend" write their characteristics in the boxes.

Colour in this celebration
of your name!

Caroline's
Favourite Book

What is your favourite book and who wrote it?

Give a brief summary of the plot.

Who is your favourite and least favourite characters in that book?

Draw a character or scene from that book.

27

Caroline's Style

What are your 3 favourite items of clothing, give each item a mark out of 10 for style and comfort.
(Like this: Ripped Jeans - C = 7 / S = 10)

1. _____

2. _____

3. _____

Describe your style in a couple of sentences or draw or stick in a picture.

What is your favourite clothing store or brand?

Imagine you are a famous fashion designer, design your favourite costume or outfit below.

Caroline's
Favourite Food & Drink

What is your favourite food or meal?

Who is your favourite cook?

What is your favourite restaurant?

What is your favourite flavour?

What is your favourite drink?

Write out below your favourite recipe, include the ingredients, cooking times and temperatures and instructions...

Recipe Name:
_____

Ingredients:

Instructions:

Caroline's
Dream
Smoothie or Milkshake

Create your dream smoothie or milkshake, what flavours ingredients and toppings would you use? You can tell a lot about a person for their smoothie or milkshake choices!

Below write out the main ingredients and toppings you would choose. Then decorate the glass picture with how it would look. It can be as simple or crazy as you like!

Ingredients:

Toppings:

33

Caroline's Animals

In this section you can write all about your pets. If you don't have a real pet, you can make one up!

Name(s)..

Type of animal(s)..

Draw a picture:

What do you love about your pet?

What is the best thing about having a pet?

What is the worst thing about having a pet?

If your pet could talk what would it say?

Caroline's

Stick in some favourite pics, either ones you took, or of you or just some pics you found or cut out...

Photoshoot

Caroline the Superhero!

What would your superhero name be?

....

What would your superpower be?

....

What would your arch nemesis be called?

....

What would their superpower be?

....

Seven things Caroline would like to do in the next year:

1

2

3

4

5

6

7

Caroline's
Favourite Game

What is your favourite game?

What is the game about?

How do you play?

How often do you play?

Who do you like to play it with?

Why is it your favourite game?

Caroline's
Favourite Film

Title

_____

What's it about?

_____

_____

_____

What do you like about it?

_____

_____

Caroline's
Dream Jar

Write or draw your favourite ever dream,
or if you want make up an interesting,
exciting or unusual dream you would like
to have!

Caroline's
Favourite Video

Describe below your favourite video or television programme.

Name

Description

What is it you like most about it?

Caroline's
Holiday

Think of your best holiday ever, either one you've been on
or your dream holiday

Draw a picture or stick in a map or a photo on the suitcase

Who did you go with?

What did you do?

What was the best
bit of your holiday?

What was your
favourite meal?

Write a postcard to a real or
imaginary friend from your holiday

Dear Future
Caroline

Write a message to Caroline in 10 years time. Your hopes, dreams, goals and ambitions.

More about Caroline...

More about Caroline...

More about Caroline...

Made in the USA
Columbia, SC
20 September 2022

67648729R00035